BUDGETING

AT YOUR

FINGER TIPS

BY ERIC GELB
CPA & MBA

BUDGETING AT YOUR FINGER TIPS
ISBN: 0-9631289-4-9

Copyright © 1994 Eric Gelb

Published by:
Career Advancement Center, Inc.
Woodmere, New York, USA

This guide contains advice about managing money, investing money and income taxes. But the use of a book is not a substitute for legal, accounting, banking, business or other professional services. Consult the appropriate professional for answers to your specific questions.

First Printing 1994

★ ★ ★ ★ ★

Other personal finance books by Eric Gelb:

**Personal Budget Planner -
A Guide for Financial Success**

**Checkbook Management -
A Guide to Saving Money**

BUDGETING AT YOUR FINGER TIPS

The word "Budget" often conjures up images of wearing a straightjacket and taking cough medicine. And, as a rule of thumb, most people avoid personal budgeting like the plague. But, a budget does not have to be painful or force you into austerity.

What is a budget?

A budget or spending plan is a tool to help you manage your money and attain your financial goals. Think of a spending plan as a compilation of your income and expenses that helps you control your cash flow to meet your expenses and save more money. This is a financial plan.

Fancy calculations and complex systems are not necessary — just an understanding of your income, expenses, and how you spend your money.

Why make a spending plan?

Establishing and maintaining a spending plan helps you manage your money, shows how much you can spend without incurring a deficit, and exposes spending habits which may prevent you from attaining your financial goals. A spending plan will help you carry out your overall financial plan and can help you avoid financial trouble.

A spending plan should be a simple system that works for you. You don't need a computer or even a detailed accountant's ledger book. As a matter of fact, long before the computer was invented, my grandparents managed their personal finances with the "Envelope System."

My grandmother kept an envelope for each spending category: food, rent, entertainment, clothes, utilities, medical costs, vacations, emergency money and savings. When grandpa brought home his paycheck, grandma divided the cash among each category and deposited the budgeted amount into the appropriate envelope. Very simple yet very efficient. What's more, their financial plan worked.

And that's what this guide is about: how to create a working spending plan to help you organize your money and manage your personal finances.

I have created a step-by-step personal finance system to help you save money and build wealth. When you complete the user-friendly worksheet and establish a financial plan, you should find that managing your finances becomes easier and your financial goals are within reach.

I look forward to hearing your thoughts and experiences. Best wishes for financial success,

Eric Gelb

c/o Career Advancement Center, Inc.
PO Box 436
Woodmere, NY 11598-0436

THE MOTIVATION

The first step towards creating a spending plan is setting financial goals. Even though goal setting is a popular buzz word today, setting goals is extremely important. Goals give you a target and an incentive to establish an overall financial plan and organize your finances. A spending plan gives you direction to manage your spending to attain your goals.

Choose one or two specific goals. The goal's importance to you is much more significant than the exact nature of the goal.

Here are a few ideas to start the process:

Build an investment portfolio
Buy a new car
Buy a house or condominium
Buy a bigger house
Pay off credit card debt
Save for retirement
Stop bouncing checks
Stop running out of money
Take a vacation

These goals represent only a few of many possible goals, and these goals may not be at the top of your list. Select your goals and write them in the space above or in the inside front cover of this guide. This will provide tangible evidence of your goal and a constant reminder of your objectives. In addition, review your goals frequently to renew your motivation to stick to your financial plan.

THE ESSENCE OF BUDGETING

Many people are surprised when they find out there are only three important points to budgeting.

1. Matching your cash outflows (spending) with your cash inflows (income),

2. Developing a realistic picture of your income and spending needs and habits, and

3. Managing your spending so you never run out of money and you attain your financial goals.

And, once you adapt the Budgeting at Your Finger Tips money management system to your own personal finances, your financial plan should be on automatic pilot. Better yet, you probably won't need to refer to the worksheet very often. Even though this system requires little continuing involvement, review your plan at least once a year and whenever your circumstances change. Otherwise, put your financial plan on automatic pilot; concentrate on the activities that interest you, and watch as your financial goals materialize.

This spending system was designed with a view towards helping you manage your money on a monthly basis. A monthly time frame is useful because people incur most of their expenses such as rent and loan payments on a monthly basis.

Alternatively, you could plan your budget on an annual basis beginning with your annual salary and convert your annual financial plan to a monthly or weekly spending plan. But a monthly plan can be more effective because your expenses might vary from month to month, and relying on averages might result in a cash shortfall in a particular month.

MAKING A WORKING SPENDING PLAN

The following paragraphs relate to the line numbers in the spending plan worksheet on pages 8 and 9.

Line 1: <u>Pretax Income</u>
Pretax income is the starting point for establishing a spending plan and calculating your spendable cash flow. Begin with your base salary, pension or social security income because your income level determines how much money you should spend on a continuing basis.

Exclude year-end bonuses or incentive compensation from your pretax income and your spending plan because these types of income are not usually guaranteed. Take a more conservative approach and base your spending on your guaranteed take-home pay; consider bonuses and incentive pay as extra compensation. This way, you should not get caught short if your bonus doesn't materialize. In addition, when you spend only your base salary (take-home pay) or less and save your bonuses and incentive compensation, you'll build more wealth.

If you want to maximize your wealth, exclude investment income from pretax income and spendable cash flow. This focuses your spending on your continuing cash flow and helps you save money for the future. When you invest your money, reinvest all the principal, interest income, and dividends to take advantage of the power of compound returns.

When planning a spending program, be realistic when forecasting your income and structuring your expenses. Most of us earn a fixed salary and therefore know how much money we receive and can allocate between spending and savings. When our income is based on commissions such as a salesperson's income, it is helpful to assume this year's income will equal last year's income, and base our spending on last year's income; any improved performance and increased compensation will be a true bonus and will seem like found money.

SPENDING PLAN WORKSHEET

		Yourself	Partner	Total
1	Pretax Income:			
2	Retirement Savings:			
3	Taxable Income:			
4	Income Taxes:			
5	Take–Home Pay:			
	Fixed Costs:			
	Automatic Savings:			
	Housing:			
	Loan Payments:			
	Car Expenses:			
	Utilities:			
	Commuting:			
6	Total Fixed Costs:			

Periodic Costs:

Insurance Premiums: _____

Medical Expenses: _____

Club/Religious/Tuition: _____

Estimated Tax Payments: _____

Automobile Repair Costs: _____

Vacations: _____

7 Total Periodic Costs: _____

8 Spendable Cash Flow: _____

9 Out-of-Pocket Spending: _____

10 Credit Card Spending: _____

11 Surplus / Deficit: _____

published by: Career Advancement Center, Inc.
Woodmere, New York USA

9

When your career is seasonal such as teaching, you may receive paychecks during part of the year only. Manage your monthly spending during the months when you receive paychecks, to save enough money for the months when you don't receive any paychecks. This should smooth your cash flow year-round.

Line 2: Retirement Savings

Unfortunately, more and more companies are reducing pension plan and post-retirement medical benefits, and social security income does not seem to cover all of our retirement needs. Therefore, it is crucial to begin saving money for our retirement, as early as possible.

The most powerful way to save money for retirement is to establish a 401(k) plan (sponsored by for-profit companies; 1993 contribution limit: $8,994); a 403(b) plan (offered by not-for-profit organizations such as hospitals and universities; 1993 contribution limit: $9,500); or an IRA account (individual retirement account; 1993 and 1994 contribution limit: $2,000). 1994 contribution limits for 401(k) and 403(b) plans are expected to increase based on the cost of living adjustment.

Qualified contributions to retirement accounts reduce your taxable income in the year of contribution (Line 2 will be a negative number), and the income accumulates tax-free until you make withdrawals. Alternatively, withdrawals from your retirement plans and retirement accounts will increase your taxable income in the year of withdrawal (Line 2 will be a positive number).

There are limits on contributions and penalties associated with withdrawals before you reach age 59½; and withdrawals become mandatory at age 70½, so consult your CPA before opening or changing a retirement account.

Line 3: Taxable Income
Pretax Income (Line 1) plus or minus Retirement Savings (Line 2). Taxable income is the amount of money on which Uncle Sam bases his income tax take.

Line 4: Income Taxes
40% multiplied by Taxable Income (Line 3). Tax rates vary based on your taxable income, but a reasonable estimate of your marginal tax rate is 40%. 40% may seem relatively high, but we pay Federal, state and local income taxes. The remainder is for social security withholding of 6.2% of the first $57,600 of 1993 wages (6.2% of the first $60,600 of 1994 wages); and medicare of 1.45% of all 1993 and 1994 wages.

Line 5: Take-Home Pay
Taxable Income (Line 3) minus Income Taxes (Line 4).

Your take-home pay is the amount of money you have available to spend; make your take-home pay your spendable cash flow or spending ceiling. This means, keep your total spending within this amount. When your spending exceeds your take-home pay, you will incur a deficit, deplete your savings or possibly resort to cash advances or high-cost credit card debt. So, structure your expenses and manage your spending so they are less than your take-home pay. This will help you avoid deficits.

Line 6: Fixed Costs
Fixed costs are expenses that people incur every month, regardless of their activities. Fixed costs generally stay constant in the near term and include housing (rent, mortgage, co-op maintenance), loan payments, car expenses (loan, lease, or garage payments), utilities (telephone, electricity), commuting costs and automatic monthly savings. Since you must pay these expenses every month, manage your other spending so you will have enough cash to cover these checks.

Do you have an automatic monthly savings plan?

Automatic monthly savings programs are important for near-term purchases such as buying a car or home, but differ from retirement savings because the deposit is in after-tax dollars, and usually, there are no income tax penalties for withdrawals. Many mutual fund families offer these savings programs where they transfer a fixed sum of money from your checking account to your mutual fund account every month, free of charge.

Consider these two mutual fund families which require monthly minimum investments but not initial minimum account balances:

Mutual Fund Family	Minimum Monthly Investment	Telephone Number
Janus Funds	$50	1-800-525-8983
Twentieth Century Investors	$25	1-800-345-2021

Automatic monthly transfers provide no-excuses saving. You save money every month, and your money works for you continuously. To maximize your wealth, elect to reinvest all interest, dividends, distributions and payouts.

Total your fixed costs on Line 6.

Line 7: Periodic Costs
Periodic costs are expenses we incur at different times throughout the year. Periodic costs include insurance premiums, medical expenses, club dues, religious contributions, tuition, estimated income tax payments, automobile repair costs, and vacations. Periodic expenses remain relatively constant from one year to the next, so you should be able to estimate these costs and set aside enough money to meet these expenses.

Total your periodic expenses on Line 7.

In order to accumulate enough cash to pay your periodic expenses on time, save 1/12th of your annual periodic costs every month. You can earn interest income until the bills come due by investing your cash in high quality money market accounts or money market mutual funds. Money market investments help you earn interest income and preserve your principal.

Do you pay for your vacations twice?

Many people unwittingly do this: they pay once for the cost of the trip and a second time for the credit card interest. To avoid this financial drain, convert vacation expenses into a periodic cost. Set your annual vacation budget and save 1/12th of your vacation budget in your money market account or money market mutual fund every month. Then you should be able to pay your vacation bill in full on time and have a second vacation on the interest saved.

Line 8: Spendable Cash Flow
Take-Home Pay (Line 5) minus Fixed Costs (Line 6) minus Periodic Costs (Line 7).

Now comes the fun part — personal spending. Spendable cash flow is the amount of money you have left over after you pay all your expenses. Keep your personal spending (Line 9 and Line 10) to less than your spendable cash flow and you should never incur a deficit.

Line 9: Out-of-Pocket Spending ("OOPs")
Out-of-pocket spending gives people the most trouble because once they withdraw money from a cash withdrawal or automated teller machine ("ATM"), the cash disappears.

1. Set a weekly cash spending budget; choose $50 or $100 or whatever your spending plan allows, and make only one ATM cash withdrawal per week. Often Sunday night or Monday morning is optimal.

2. Track your OOPs spending for at least one or two months; buy a note pad and record every expenditure you make.

Once you see how you spend your money, make changes to attain your financial goals. Reduce your out-of-pocket expenses and spending to fit within your spending plan rather than resort to extra cash withdrawals or borrowing from credit cards.

Line 10: Credit Card Spending

Credit cards make it easy for people to spend money, especially with cable television shopping services and mail order catalogs. In addition, credit card companies offer cardholders the option to pay only a fraction of the bill — the minimum payment. And this leads to high cost credit card debt.

Keep your credit card spending to fit within your spendable cash flow and certainly an amount you can pay off in full, every month. If you have credit card debt or cannot pay your credit card bill in full, STOP using your credit cards until you pay off the debt. Then, use credit cards carefully, or use cash.

Line 11: Surplus/Deficit

Spendable Cash Flow (Line 8) minus OOPs (Line 9) minus Credit Card Spending (Line 10).

Surplus/Deficit is the bottom line — the difference between your income and total spending. If Line 11 is positive, you spent less than your income (at least on paper); your financial plan should work, and you should attain your financial goals.

If Line 11 is negative and you stick with your spending habits, most likely, you will incur a deficit. To create a surplus, review your spending plan worksheet and decide how you can lower your fixed costs, periodic costs, out-of-pocket spending or credit card spending. In addition, you can increase your take-home pay by landing a part-time job.

Summary
So that's <u>Budgeting At Your Finger Tips</u>. No straightjackets.
No cough medicine. Just simple tools to help you manage your
money and attain your financial goals.

First, set one or two important personal financial goals. Then,
make a spending plan and implement it. This means structuring
your expenses and adjusting your OOPs and credit card spending
to fit within your spending program.

Finally, don't resort to additional cash withdrawals or borrowing
from credit cards; rather shrink your expenses and spending to
fit within your spending plan. When you stick with your
financial plan, you should always have money, avoid incurring
deficits, and be able to attain your financial goals.

I look forward to hearing your thoughts and experiences. Best
wishes for financial success,

Eric Gelb

★ ★ ★ ★ ★

With Eric Gelb's personal finance books, you will discover more wealth-building
strategies and money-saving tactics:

Personal Budget Planner
A Guide for Financial Success

Checkbook Management
A Guide to Saving Money

INC. magazine: "Personal Budget Planner is exhaustive in its efforts to help readers gain
control of their finances."

THE BOOKWATCH: "Personal Budget Planner blends anecdotes with solid examples.
Financial tables encourage know-how rather than vague speculations and theories."

BOOKLIST: "Personal Budget Planner offers straightforward advice on personal finance
and budget planning."

CAREER ADVANCEMENT CENTER ORDER FORM

☎ Telephone Orders: Call our credit card ordering center toll-free: 1-800-669-0773. Please have your Mastercard or Visa card ready. Minimum credit card order amount before shipping charge: $6.50.

🕐 FAX Orders: 515-472-3186.

☒ By Mail: Career Advancement Center, Box 436, Woodmere, NY 11598-0436.

Please send the following books. I understand that I may return any books for a full refund for any reason — no questions asked.

Title	Qty	Price	Total
Personal Budget Planner by Eric Gelb		$19.95	
Checkbook Management by Eric Gelb		$6.50	
Budgeting at your Finger Tips by Eric Gelb		$3.50	
Teach Your Child the Value of Money by Harold & Sandy Moe		$7.95	
High Impact Resumes & Letters by Dr. Ron Krannich & Dr. Wm. Banis		$12.95	
Total Order Price:			
Shipping & Handling:			$3.00
Sales Tax (NYS & NYC residents):			
Total:			

Name:	
Address:	
City/State/Zip Code:	

Credit Card signature:	
Card # & Expiration Date:	

Please allow 4-6 weeks for delivery.